A GOOD KISS

ALSO BY MARSHALL STEWART BALL

Kiss of God

A
GOOD
KISS

*The Wisdom of a
Listening Child*

Marshall Stewart Ball

POCKET BOOKS
New York London Toronto Sydney Singapore

POCKET BOOKS, a division of Simon & Schuster, Inc.
1230 Avenue of the Americas, New York, NY 10020

ISBN: 0-7434-3462-5

First Pocket Books hardcover printing October 2001

10   9   8   7   6   5   4   3   2   1

POCKET and colophon are registered trademarks of
Simon & Schuster, Inc.

For information regarding special discounts
for bulk purchases, please contact
Simon & Schuster Special Sales at 1-800-456-6798
or business@simonandschuster.com

Designed by Jaime Putorti

Printed in the U.S.A.

To good, balanced,
thoughtful and loving Dad,
Marshall dares to master
the good marvelous Love
you give to me.

CONTENTS

Acknowledgments
ix

Preface by Troylyn Ball
xiii

ONE
Good Kisses
1

TWO
Daring to Be Good
23

THREE
No Greater Gift
45

❦ CONTENTS ❦

FOUR

Balanced Marshall Listens

65

FIVE

Finding Great Victory

91

SIX

Marshall's Rich Sweet Life

121

SEVEN

Good Thoughts of Love

145

EIGHT

Good Kisses from Good Friends

173

ACKNOWLEDGMENTS

MARSHALL

That Marshall gives thanks to Love, that takes in wonderful thoughts defining my thought.

Marshall thanks marvelous thorough fine Mama, good Grandmother, sweet Cindy, giving Tricia, loving Hill and Quin, kissing Coulton, thinking Luke, magnificent good Dad. Marshall loves you giving, loving Laurence. Balanced Kyle definitely loves. Good loving James, each thoughtful day names you daring listener. Marshall is kissing finely you all.

TROYLYN

I would like to give special thanks to my mother, Louise Wigginton, who on a daily basis assists Marshall with his mail and provides immeasurable love and support to the entire family. To my father, Don Wigginton, if he were with us today, I would say, "You were right. It wasn't what Marshall needed to learn from us, but what we needed to learn from him. You would be proud but not surprised by the gifts of Marshall."

My special thanks also to Jaynan and Jerry Ball, Marshall's grandparents, for understanding and appreciating our family. I'll always be grateful for the dedication to Marshall of Laurence A. Becker, Ph.D., Dr. Keith Turner, Bill Webster, James Bell, Th.M., Jo Ogden, Mahnaz and Hadi Parhikhteh, Gerald Fitzgibbon, Bob Beltran, Cindy Cashman, John Jordan, David Hanley, Dr. David Ruiz, Dr. Jerry Hudson, Meg LaBorde, and Lois "Lovely" Johnson.

Without the countless hours of administrative help from Aunt Cindy, my sister, we certainly would not have been as timely in getting *A Good Kiss* out to the world.

Thank you all for loving Marshall.

And to those who have taken care of me over the years, Rosie Chambers, Nancy deJuan, Carmen Oppenheimer, Carol Swanteson, Aan Coleman, Jennifer Fronk, Lynn Meredith, and Cricket Wilson. I can't tell you what your love and support has meant.

And most importantly, to my adoring husband, and

my children's dedicated, loving father. Charlie, you give us all the strength to go day to day, to tackle the physical as well as emotional challenges we face. The moment I saw you I knew you were the one for me, and in the second moment, I knew you would be the father of my children.

PREFACE

By Troylyn Ball

From the moment Marshall was first placed on my chest and I could see his delicately curved lips and round baby face, I knew my life would never be the same. It would take years for me to fully appreciate the blessing that Marshall would bring to my life. He would teach me patience. His struggle would become my passion and his life would become my gift. But first he would make me strong.

As perfectly formed as our first child was, Marshall failed to thrive. He couldn't nurse as other babies did, and that left me feeling a failure only two months into motherhood. Even fattened on formula it became clear that Marshall wasn't developing as children usually do. He wasn't making the sounds that infants usually make. He wouldn't hold his head up and he couldn't crawl. We decided to love him anyway.

Marshall's father, Charlie, and I decided that we would not limit our son in any way. After all, no one had been able to tell us what was wrong with Marshall. What if he was listening? What about the Helen Kellers and the Stephen Hawkings of the world? Suppose no one had listened to them?

Charlie and I were crushed by the idea that Marshall would not grow up to be the ideal son we had dreamed about during pregnancy. Nevertheless, we poured ourselves into loving and nurturing this fragile, serene child. We read volumes to Marshall. We talked to him about everything. We took him to zoos, to museums and botanical gardens. We went on picnics by rivers and creeks. We backpacked with him in the mountains. We traveled from Maine to California, stopping any place that we thought would be interesting or educational. And, we were rewarded. Not by Marshall's bubbling baby words,—he never spoke—but by the expression in his eyes and his rare, precious smile. We treasure that smile more than anything.

An then when our beautiful son was three and a half we learned that he was indeed listening. With Marshall sitting on my lap one December day, I happened to hold a new toy up to his eye level. I was showing Marshall the large yellow buttons that made animal sounds, when all of a sudden he leaned forward and pushed a button with his forehead. I was amazed. Marshall had never used his hands to play so I knew he was making a conscious movement to activate the toy. I asked him if he could push the same button again. The sound of the cat's meow was music to my ears. Brimming with happiness I asked him to push the dog button, the lion, and the goat. He did.

Life changed immensely that rewarding day. Within a matter of weeks Marshall was making choices about everything. He would tell me what color of shirt he wanted to wear or what kind of food he wanted for dinner. We would show him different colors and he would identify them. When we presented pictures of animals he would touch his forehead to the animal we asked for. In fact, we rather quickly began using picture symbols depicting nearly any kind of activity or choice of things. His ability to correctly answer questions was not so surprising—not if you considered that his intelligence was normal. But, as we were soon to learn, Marshall's ability far exceeded that of the average child.

Marshall was already enrolled in an early childhood program in public school, but I became alarmed when I realized that his teachers might be underteaching him. After all, Marshall still sat quietly, rather uninvolved in his surroundings. He didn't play with toys, and he didn't appear to look toward any place in particular. It was only when his picture symbols or items were placed in front of him that he became excited, an excitement he showed by kicking his feet. I decided the last thing that teachers needed was a parent who was trying to tell them about their job, but I was passionate about Marshall's teacher understanding him, so I began my search for a professional who could evaluate him. Fortunately I found Dr. Keith Turner at The University of Texas at Austin, who had a special interest in disabled children who were misdiagnosed because standard testing often does not work with the severely handicapped. Dr. Turner agreed to evaluate Marshall, but said he wanted the evaluation to be done in our home because that was where Marshall was most comfortable. On Dr. Turner's first visit, Marshall was videotaped correctly identifying animals from a book. He surprised us by showing us the words lion, giraffe, and snake. Importantly, Marshall also sat in Dr. Turner's lap and identified pictures for him. It wasn't surprising that Marshall felt comfortable with Dr. Turner; only minutes after arriving, Dr. Turner was on the floor with Marshall talking to him as if he understood everything. In other words, treating him like a normal child.

Dr. Turner became a friend. It was so wonderful finding this kind man who appreciated Marshall as much as we did. Over the next year or so Dr. Turner spent many hours videotaping Marshall. He developed a protocol for Marshall, giving him thirty seconds to answer questions before they would be marked wrong. He taped Marshall working on games and problems with his speech therapist, Dee Dee Ramos Barrera. And eventually, with the help of Dee Dee, a standardized multiple choice test was modified to fit the now familiar two-by-two-inch block format, so that Marshall could use his head to answer the test questions. The results were amazing. Marshall basically tested out of this standardized test. He was two standard deviations above normal. A five-and-a-half-year-old who was on at least a third-grade level. By this time none of us were surprised by the incredible gift in an unexpected package.

I then began to notice that Marshall would try to tap on his display boards with his right hand. I told him that if he wanted to try using his hand to indicate choices I would try to help him. So began the process of learning how to use the homemade alphabet board. I decided that I would use his familiar two-by-two-inch letters and arrange them in the order that he had learned them. In hindsight, it might have been better to arrange them like a keyboard, but I thought it would be logical for him to find the letters as he had learned them in the alphabet.

Marshall had a significant amount of muscle weakness, so I decided to try supporting his elbow in my palm, relieving some of the work of his upper arm. In other words, I was creating a personal fulcrum from which he could pivot his elbow and move his lower arm to point to a letter. At the beginning I would just ask Marshall to try to touch a particular letter like the A or G. After a while, however, Marshall figured out that if he shifted his weight or leaned over in one direction he could help move his arm to the part of the board he wanted to reach. And quite by chance I discovered that if I gave Marshall some upward pressure from his elbow into his shoulder he would be able to push out with his arm more easily. Many years later I learned that the upward pressure I was giving Marshall is actually called proprioceptive feedback and is a frequently used treatment in therapy. Evidently the pressure in Marshall's shoulder would trigger a signal to the brain, which would then send a signal back to the muscle allowing it to push out. Even today I'm not sure how this feedback system really works, but I do know it helped Marshall become more accurate with his pointing.

Since Marshall was, by this time, an accomplished reader, it was not surprising that he could already spell fairly well. When he didn't know how to spell a word he would point to the first couple of letters and then he would tap the Q, which meant question. I would then figure out that he was trying to spell a new word and would encourage him to just try to spell it the best that he could. Sometimes the word was easily deduced and yet, at other times, we might sit for an hour struggling over a word like "jagged" or "juxtaposed." Within weeks of using the new alphabet board Marshall was writing in sentences and even creating poetic lines. One of Marshall's first poems, "Altogether Lovely," was written within two months of learning how to use the alphabet board. Marshall still receives letters from people telling him how this poem inspires them.

Once Marshall found his voice, which came through his finely chiseled delicate fingers, our life changed radically. Never again would we wonder about his thoughts. Now we were amazed by them. The understanding that he seemed to naturally possess was inspiring, if not shocking. He became our teacher, the one we sought on nearly every issue of importance to our family, that others sought for guidance and solace. I wish I could share here just how Marshall has changed our lives, but the story is too great to be contained in these few pages. I can say that Marshall, through his simple profound words, has touched hundreds of thousands of lives around the world. After the release of *Kiss of God,* a book that was compiled for his father as a Christmas gift, Marshall began receiving thousands of letters and e-mails which he attempted to respond to as he could. In fact, his life became a daily ritual of listening to letters and writing the many who sought his words. When asked how he felt about all the attention he has received on national television, in magazines like *Time* and *People,* in newspaper articles and in radio interviews, Marshall succinctly wrote "Words teach."

Marshall has asked me to help him teach, to help him give love. I am compelled to do so. You will find conversations in this book where he asks me to help him and where he asks others to help. Just today some family friends, Jim and Kathy Field, dropped by and Marshall, after inscribing several books for their friends, said he wanted to talk to them. He very directly asked them to give love to others, particularly to "battered man."

In these pages, Marshall's thoughts are shown in block print while questions or comments by others or me will be seen in italics. I'm certain, as you read, you will realize Marshall's message, whether by miracle or gift, will speak directly to you. And you will know that he wants you to teach also. He wants you to give A Good Kiss. That is, kissing with your heart.

To Good Thinkers

To catapult intelligent good thinking,
this angel takes you to that good good thought,
taught with a good kiss.

ONE

GOOD KISSES

Kisses come when you read each word.

*K*isses are Marshall's way of giving. He defines a kiss as "God's thought." Marshall kisses each of us with God's thoughts, a lovely salutation. These thoughts disarm us, undress us, and move us—often to tears. Marshall kisses the wounded to healing. He kisses the strong to arrest busyness so that they can listen to what God is telling them. Though he is silent, his words speak in high intensity to those who would have ears to hear. What a wonderful blessing to receive a kiss from one so pure, so lovely, so delicate.

Marshall does not stop there. He challenges each of us to become good kissers. He wants us to pass God's thoughts to others.

This conversation took place with Marshall's mother on a fall afternoon. As usual, Marshall shares his happiness and thoughts in a lyrical, touching way.

Good good Mama, that Marshall is happy. Would that Marshall kiss that good Mama?

You always kiss me with your thoughts.

Kisses give meager candid Marshall good balance.

While sitting in the Thoughtful House, Marshall's stone cottage across the lawn from his home, he wrote this letter to his dad imploring him to help Marshall give A Good Kiss.

Dad,

Marshall thinks that you manage to make good Marshall happy. Balance that marvelous Marshall thought and give to many. Marshall is always giving Love. Marshall can give *A Good Kiss,* to marshall good giving to thinkers. You can help.

Good Dad, Marshall makes you that giving good Dad. Give magnificently Marshall Love. Marshall thinks you give with understanding. Can you give *A Good Kiss?* Marshall understands that good stations us leaving order. What a grand plan.

Marshall gives you love.

The Noel Foundation asked Marshall to write the invocation for their awards ceremony. The Noel Foundation is an international organization dedicated to entrepreneurial vision, economic development, and peace worldwide. They were recognizing significant women of the twentieth century who have made a difference through their leadership and support of action-oriented projects, including Rosa Parks, Audrey Hepburn, Judge Navanethem Pillay of South Africa, and Dr. Hadassa Digani of Israel. He wrote this letter to Noel Hentschel, the founder.

That Good Noel,

You find the Love that Marshall would see. Giving more Love takes magnificent thought. Your pure, caring thought helps. Would you joyfully give caring kisses to marvelous, magnificent, poor people? Would you take time to kiss lovely, thoughtful, poor people with me?

Marshall

*I*n *this conversation with his mother, Marshall wrote the line "Never think Love needs," which became one of her favorites.*

Is there anything you want to tell me?

Yes. Great nice good Marshall sets meagerly, caring fine thoughts, to tell the loving, real Marshall frees.

I've been very busy all day working on things for you. There is so much happening now. How do you feel about all this media being interested in you?

Love finds Marshall.

Do you need me to be here more during the day?

Great Marshall teaches. You question my wonderful teaching?

What do you mean?

Never think Love needs. That Marshall thinks Love teaches. Room takes Marshall to Love.

What do you mean by room?

That room teaches. That room I give to thought.

Does that mean when I'm not here you have time to think?

That Marshall loves you.

I love you Marshall. As you teach me, your explanations teach others.

That sweet thought loves you.

Good meager beautiful Love gives.

Marshall's thought is to happily give
real good fine love to marvelous thinkers.

*M*inutes after Marshall appeared on a national television show, Marshall's mother received a call from a representative of People magazine. This conversation with Hillary Hylton took place a couple of weeks later when she came to interview Marshall and his parents.

Marshall, you seem to have some favorite words. Do you choose them because they have a special meaning to you?

Yes.

What is one of your favorite words?

Taming. Marshall loves the idea that thoughts can tame people.

Marshall, why did you name your book Kiss of God?

Good God finely pleases listening poor people with generous kisses. Teach good answers with pure thoughts, like teaching with kisses.

Will you write another book?

Each great day Marshall will write to all of the loving sweet thinkers.

*M**arshall's first book signing took place in Austin, Texas and was widely attended by fans and the media including CNN,* People *magazine and other local press. Several well-known Texas poets including Peggy Lynch, poet laureate, American University of Paris, Byron Kocen and Frank Pool of the Austin International Poetry Society, read Marshall's poems. After the event, Marshall happily shared his thoughts with Aunt Cindy, family friend Peter Nitshdale, and his mother.*

What did you think about the book signing today? How did you feel?

I attain love. That good Marshall is happy. Room takes in talent, balancing that good fine Marshall with that thought, announcing that good Marshall would take time to give kisses.

Connie and Robert Rust, friends of the family, asked for a copy of Kiss of God for friends of theirs whose thirteen-year-old son had just died of cancer. Their son, Zane, after a long and valiant battle, voluntarily requested that his medication be stopped. Two days later he died. Marshall wrote this message to Zane's parents while sitting on the porch at Mearwild just after sunset. This evening will be remembered by all present for many years. As the sun began to sink behind the mountains, three large bucks slowly ambled into the eastern meadow as if beckoned by the cello sonatas of Bach, which played softly for Marshall. These elegant, wild animals came boldly down the meadow nearly to the house. This mystical encounter was the prelude to Marshall drafting this letter by candlelight.

To Zane's Parents,

Marshall gives good Marshall kisses and cares greatly that quiet Zane gives that good Good God that real pure trusting nice Love. Battered man, there in good Good God's arms, would take justice to Love. Are you in spirit with Marshall and good Zane? Take understanding, giving careful thought, managing Marshall joy. The Marshall nicely gives you that Kiss of God.

Fine Love gives kisses.
Take kisses and share His Love.
The good kiss feels the love you give.
Feelings go now to you,
and you are blessed.

Good understanding stops turmoil.
Teach the children
that richness takes Love
that thoughts can teach Love.
Marshall loves children.
Marvelous thinking understands
real joy is teaching Love.
Marshall loves you.

We need to find perfect love in all.

T W O

DARING TO BE GOOD

Daring answers make balance present.

This chapter is a collection of Marshall's writings about his daring to be "Good Marshall." These poems, thoughts, and conversations explore personal issues, such as how Marshall feels about not being able to speak, why he writes, how he views himself, and what he hopes to accomplish.

While talking with his mother, Marshall explains why he writes books. His purpose, to teach and help people, is not motivated by fame, but always by love.

Marshall, why do you want to write books?

Nice thought teaches that great Love takes too much time. You can teach pure old thoughts, finely through words that Love.

It sounds as if teaching one on one is too time consuming, and that you feel you can touch more people through your books.

Marshall is a tame thinker. Can Marshall tame with words? That is my nice reason to write.

After the release of Kiss of God *in the Fall of 1999, Marshall began receiving thousands of letters and e-mails. Despite the recognition, Marshall always remained calm and purposeful. This conversation explores a question that came up several times in letters.*

How do you feel about receiving so much mail?

That Marshall thinks good, poor, thoughtful people know that Love that Marshall gives, is to love real wonderful God.

Is there anything you want to tell me?

Yes. That Marshall takes that thinker to God.

I think you do. Many people have asked what you mean when you write, "Marshall has been here for millions of lifetimes."

I think Marshall makes Love that good thought. Each day takes me to Good God. The real thinkers Marshall loves, take ideas taught to meager listening people. Marshall loves you.

I love you too, sweetheart.

Sweet to give teaching kisses.

What about "millions of lifetimes?"

Marshall is giving thought to the question. Be a good Mama. Would you write that good ideas know sweetness takes good fortunate, thinking, nearly thoughtful, poor people to God? Worlds take time to teach. Harmony takes good time to teach. Would you make worlds for teaching? God gave worlds lovingly to teach.

Fine and kind answers
beautifully dare the giver
teaching Love.

Marshall enjoys using words in atypical ways. Here, in a conversation about "daring" people, Marshall uses the word "last" and defines its meaning.

You think a lot about daring people.

Yes. Daring people kindly take a meager attitude, marshalling great thoughts and last Marshall meagerly with love.

Is "last" the word you want to use?

Yes.

What does it mean?

A love that greatly binds.

Can I look up "last" in the dictionary?

Yes.

It says "last" can mean to fasten or fit.

Yes.

*M*arshall sets a high standard for everyone. These *thoughts both challenge and inspire his parents.*

Good Marshall dares
good mama and dad
to be magnificent thinking
great giving rich thinkers.

Teaching gives love
and caring Marshall gives Love
through loving parents.

This conversation took place with Marshall's mother at 3:00 A.M. in Marshall's bedroom. As he began to write, it became clear that Marshall had been lying in bed thinking about some very important things. Afterward, his mother was very happy to have had the conversation, despite the late hour.

You are wide awake. Is there something you want to tell me?

Yes, love you. Marshall kisses that Mama. That Marshall understands, daring to interrupt teachings of the old teachers would take me, Marshall, to matter. That real sweet teacher finds beautiful, caring, lovely friends that meagerly love.

Where are you finding these friends?

The caring friends will live the beautiful thinking that Love gives.

Do you want to go back to bed?

Would you love each day that Marshall?

Yes, of course I will. Will you tell me when you are tired of doing interviews?

Yes, I feel like teaching takes to lovely poor people the answers.

What about the interviews?

Love you. Please, Marshall needs to undertake talking to people.

That is happening on the website.

That Marshall thinks teaching takes good time. Teaching may take the media.

Marshall, I worry about you.

Marshall loves you. Teaching has very teachable thinking caring followers. Love would take fine teaching to bad thinkers.

I understand what you are saying. Do you want to go to bed?

That Marshall loves you.

I love you Marshall.

Teaching nicely
Kissing quietly
Loving you.

Thank you Marshall.

That Marshall materialized making
God's thoughts and ideas
greatly taught.

*M**aking use of an uncommon word "garron," Marshall explains what he hopes to accomplish with* A Good Kiss. *Garron is defined in* Webster's Unabridged Dictionary *as "cut; akin to short, or a small, sturdy workhorse." Marshall says it means "feeling thoughts."*

Why do you want to write books, Marshall?

Marshall gives that eating rich listener good ideas to feast upon.

How do you feel about the book you are working on?

Daring Marshall might arrange marvelously to make *A Good Kiss* balanced, giving, caring. The purpose, gorgeous that quietly dares, forcing grand garron that lovingly teaches.

This was a conversation with Marshall's Grandmother Louise, who is affectionately called GM. The temptations referenced are the temptations of Jesus just prior to his public ministry. Marshall's grandmother asks him his thoughts on this event in the life of Christ. As always, Marshall points to dependence on God for victory. Marshall leads the listener to an ever closer walk with God.

What do you think about the temptations of Christ?

A magic feeling of Good God. Yes, Jesus was tempted. He knew Good God would ready him for his task. Going to Good God gives us power.

Time is the good we do.

THREE

No Greater Gift

Giving leaves nothing to chance.

Marshall's concept of giving has always been a matter of giving from the heart. Giving ideas and love expressed through words has been his focus for so many years, that these are the only gifts he gives, and all that he asks of others. Marshall gently shapes those who would listen, and by doing so changes their perspective about such a simple thing as a gift.

M*arshall is a great giver, not of things, but of thoughts. On Father's Day, he wrote these comforting lines to his father.*

Good good good
fine teaching Dad,
you teach me to love.
Would you see
that Marshall
good and happy
just like you?

*A*s is his practice, Marshall wrote these lines to his mother on her birthday. No gift was greater.

To Good Mama,

Mama knows that Marshall would give you nice grand thoughts to open wide the magnificent wonders that thankful thought would give.

You nicely wake up Marshall. You have taken that Marshall happily to good thanks. You taught me to meagerly write. Thank you. Thank you. That Marshall materializes to tame thought.

Marshall is loving you.

*M*arshall wrote this to his grandmother Louise when he was seven.

Good GM,

Good Marshall thinks you take me to Good.
Good takes Marshall to knowing God.
That Good clearly became my thought.
That knowledge did greatly give
Marshall that will
dear God needed me to undertake
that would teach good Marshall to love.
I need to manifest that good
God gives.
That God makes Marshall thankful to grow.
That good Marshall loves you.
That Marshall undertakes love
to interest others in Good.
Have you given me a good gift?
That needs no clear answer.
Can good Marshall teach Good to great love?
I greatly attempt seeing a magnificent thing.
GM, I love you.

Marshall Stewart Ball

When Marshall was asked what he wanted to give his dad for his birthday, he wrote, "I feel that he cares greatly for each Marshall thought." He then wrote this letter.

Great Dad,

Teaching good Luke to Love, you till marvelously the knowledge that Marshall leaves. Marshall is thanking you, kissing you.

I love that great caring Dad.

Marshall

For Christmas, Marshall gave Aunt Cindy her favorite gift, a letter of love.

Good Cindy,

That Marshall loves you. Take Love to listening poor people. Kiss listening poor lovely people. Would you take that Good Kiss? I please that Good God, loving poor people. Would you?

Listening dearly,
Marshall

*J*ust before Christmas, Marshall wrote this letter to his grandmother Louise, with the intention of having his mother transcribe it into a little journal he had given his grandmother several years earlier. This accomplished, the journal was wrapped and placed under the tree as a surprise.

Fine GM,

I love teaching you! Caring thoughts make sweet Love greatly known. Would you love sweet people with me? Take sweet words Marshall really loves, carry that Love to others. I feel that you love.

Marshall loves you.

When Marshall was asked what he wanted to give his dad for Christmas, he spelled "a sweet kind poem."

Dear Thoughtful Dad,

Kiss that Marshall.
I teach you
to make righteous,
fine, beautiful decisions.
Lovely thorough Love frees.
Love pours sweetly,
taming, teaching,
kissing nicely.

Loving you,
Good Caring Marshall

TAKE TIME

The hour needs your love.
Time takes us to a good thought.
Make time now to help others.
Giving good will make you happy.
Make a time to love all things.
The hour needs your love.

Going to God happens when you give Love.

Listen, feelings of Love are the finest.

FOUR

BALANCED
MARSHALL
LISTENS

Angels make us listen.

Over the years, Marshall has always encouraged the listener to seek balance. Through this state of balance and with a listening heart true understanding may be found. As a child, Marshall wrote "my harmony prevails to free," and as a teenager, he continues his mission.

*I*n this conversation, Marshall describes himself as "balanced," meaning balanced in his thought. Although his physical ability seems limited, he always sees himself as complete and never complains about his condition. Marshall defines balanced as "finding a happy medium."

Marshall, I love sitting with you on my lap. It makes it easy for me to kiss your cheek. Is there anything you want to talk about?

Are the sweet listeners really daring Marshall?

What do you mean?

Balanced Marshall listens well, and listeners find Marshall in all good thoughts.

I love the way you see yourself as balanced. You know many people would at first glance see you as unbalanced, needing help in ways that they can't imagine.

This conversation took place with Debra Duncan in Houston, Texas for her television show.

What lessons do you think are the most important to learn?

Take thoughts that teach balanced thinking. Understand Marshall purely loves.

You say grown-ups have a lot to learn from children. I talk to a lot of people. What advice do you have for them?

Fine, caring Debra, you take sweet Marshall's lovely caring thought. I feel like caring Debra teaches that love to listeners.

Can you teach meager people to love?

Marshall loves you.

I love you back.

That Marshall loves that thoughtful thinking taker, teaching understanding to others.

Who is the thoughtful thinking taker?

Good Debra. That good Debra takes teaching Marshall lovingly to others. Thank you, candid, daring, caring Debra.

As Marshall's home, Listener's Hill, was being remodeled, several close friendships developed between Marshall and the carpenters. Cord Steele, the project manager, photographed Marshall and it is his photo that was used on the inside cover of Kiss of God. Phil Serotta, a project carpenter, continually brought books and careful insights to the family's home.

Marshall, do you have anything you would like to say to Phil? You know how much he loves to read; he is always bringing books over to share with us. Perhaps you could explain to him why you like to write.

Love takes too much time. Love needs fine words, lovingly to give understanding.

When you say love takes too much time, what do you mean?

Good love takes time for good targeting. Carefully giving love, teaching greatly, takes sweet good written words. Fine words that teach would take careful listening thinkers wonderfully to understanding.

H*ere, Marshall answers simple questions with typically unique insight.*

How do we listen?

To listen you give understanding to kind poor people.

Do you want to tell me anything else?

Teach the good poor people to love.

Often when Marshall is picked up and his communication board is placed in front of him, he begins writing instantly. On this occasion, he was asked a question that many have wanted answered. As often happens, he gives responsibility back to the listener.

It's beautiful sitting here with you looking out your bedroom window. I'm glad this is where we put the writing desk your grandmother Nan gave you.

That good, good poor nice thought is taking that Marshall sweetly to my knowledgeable God. Marshall loves you.

People often ask if you hear God?

That Marshall loves each good and sweet day. That God raises his voice to take good Marshall to rich fine understanding. Would you take understanding that Marshall has, talk to others?

Marshall received an e-mail from an Internet friend telling him about the conflict in the Balkans and that people around the world were coming together in prayer for one minute at a particular time. Marshall's grandmother Louise and Aunt Cindy made sure they set aside some time in Marshall's schedule to join the world in prayer. After their moment in silence Marshall wrote these words.

Marshall feels like God was here.
The quiet was God.
Thoughts need quiet to hear God.
I love to be quiet
and hear God.

Prior to an interview, a reporter called Marshall's mother and asked her to have Marshall answer this question.

A reporter is coming over in an hour and she wants me to ask you, "What is the meaning of life?" Do you have an answer?

Yes. Marshall kisses you.

Are you writing that to her or me?

Love you.

I think life balances. That Marshall understands that balance pleases that kissing Good God. That Marshall pleases. Marshall thinks life loves pleasing Good God.

J ulie Bonnin of the Austin American-Statesman *wrote a beautiful, three-page story about Marshall. During her interview, she asked Marshall how he felt about being nonverbal. She was surprised by his answer.*

What do you see yourself doing in ten years?

In ten years a Good Marshall would teach. That Marshall pleases thinking understanding children of Good God.

What do you think about not being able to talk?

That Marshall will be a good talker with that Good God. Would you talk with Good God with your voice? Would talking make you think? Good God loves talking to us.

ANGELS

Wise angels hear.
Wise angels listen.
Wise angels know feelings.
Always give Love.
Marshall feels seeing angels.
Will you?

WISDOM COMES

Quietly the children listen
Wisdom comes quietly
Feelings quietly listen
Reverently listen
Going to God
Answers
Wisdom

*O*n this day, what started as a conversation turned into a poem. Marshall is often spontaneous in his writing, taking the listener to what he wants to give.

*What a gorgeous day it is. The wildflowers are bloom-
ing like crazy now. How are you feeling?*

Each day that love grows making room, and calling
my fine home, that sweet happy inspiring home. I
feel like writing.

THRICE

Look for poor me.
Can meager poor thoughts
talk to me,
talk to you?
Can I get great knowledge
talking?
Can talking make that knowledge
teach?
Talking giving good
knowledge,
greatly talks through me,
talks
beautifully for me.
Thrice
talks to me.
Can I talk like thrice?

Is the Webster's Unabridged Dictionary *definition of "thrice" what you intend—"in a threefold manner or degree, to a high degree; fully, repeatedly—used as an intensive"?*

I love you.

CARING FEELINGS

Real peace comes when we listen
to good thoughts.
We begin to hear God.
Is the unity of man evidenced in wisdom?
Wisdom needs love.
Real desires come when we listen.
Kindness finds a good peace.
Can we give kindness?
Peace will come when we love.
Give Love!

When God comes,
He speaks softly.

FIVE

FINDING GREAT VICTORY

Will you victoriously listen with me?

To Marshall, victory is obtained when understanding is given and received by good, caring people. His view of victory has nothing to do with defeat and everything to do with giving love. Here he explains that this ultimate victory takes time and the important thing is that we make time to listen.

I n classic Marshall fashion, this conversation covered many ideas, and left his mother with a joyful heart. It is her earnest desire for Marshall to be happy, and when he wrote, "Try loving Marshall's sweet life that is made to understand joy . . . ," she truly felt uplifted and grateful.

That Marshall needs to give my book to caring people real soon.

Why real soon?

Because Marshall knows poor, sweet people that I love, greatly take that understanding to good, caring, nice people.

So, you believe that people who read your book will take the understanding in the book to other people?

That definitely nicely will find, daring Marshall making a great victory.

Do you mind that people are initially interested in you because of your age and condition?

That love gives the taker the most.

I'm not sure I completely understand. Can you explain more?

Would you dare to give fine Love Marshall happily teaches, with a good thinker who can talk? That will not give a good beautiful listening picture. Try loving Marshall's sweet life that is made to understand joy, nicely taking thoughts to sweet people.

It seems that you feel good about your life.

That Marshall understands the victory takes sweet beautiful marvelous time. Marshall would make time to know victory.

You often speak of victory. What is it about victory that is so important?

Caring good Marshall each day teaches that a caring person dearly attempts finely to see Love. Can Love dearly bring fine victory?

Listen, feelings of Love are the finest.

That meager Marshall
knows that magnificent good
good God.

Meager Marshall would right that wrong.

After some investigation, Marshall's parents learned that if they wanted to help Marshall get his book out to people, they needed to find a distributor. It was decided this could possibly be accomplished by going to Book Expo of America, a large convention of booksellers and buyers. Having no experience in the book world, Marshall's parents were a little apprehensive about their chance for success. Despite their concerns, Marshall remained calm and positive, he knew that Kiss of God would help people.

Are you feeling good about taking Kiss of God *to the Book Expo? You know we are hoping to find a book distributor there who will help distribute* Kiss of God *to the bookstores.*

Yes, that Marshall knows you love the Marshall. That happy *Kiss of God* takes Marshall to victory. That opens Love Marshall wants to give. I love you. Be a good mama, take my thoughtful *Kiss of God* and teach good Marshall's thoughts to Marshall's thoughtful loving thinkers.

Marshall, I'm not the one teaching, you are.

You can take thoughts that Marshall gives.

I'm happy to do that, but I want you involved to the extent it is possible.

Can that understanding take you, giving me my voice to arrive at Marshall's purpose?

What do you mean?

You are Marshall's lovely sweet voice.

Wanting to make sure Marshall was comfortable with her upcoming surgery and needing his thoughts, Marshall's mother had this conversation with him. As always, Marshall expresses no fear and gives her a simple, poignant truth.

Marshall, do you know that I have surgery tomorrow?

Yes.

Are you worried?

Wonderful Mama, bad man worries. That pleasing understanding surgeon takes kind matter to my good, good teacher. Marshall, the victorious, takes good to that surgeon. Teaching surgeons take Mama real safely to Marshall's understanding.

Thank you for giving me the simple thought "bad man worries." I know I will be able to remember it.

During a lesson with his science and math tutors, Hadi and Mahnaz, Marshall is given a lesson on parallel lines. He, in return, gives Hadi and Mahnaz something to think about.

Do you have a definition for parallel lines?

Parallel lines make a road to infinity.

Two lines that have the same slope are parallel.

Yes.

What is the relationship between two perpendicular lines?

They never get to infinity.

Math is so pure.

God uses math to tell man how to have harmony.

What is infinity?

Where two parallel lines meet.

Who is teaching whom?

This was originally Marshall's response to an e-mail from Barbara of Nebraska. She stated that she could imagine the love with which Marshall danced "with the Lord of (his) heart," and asked if he played with Him "as a dear friend in the purest of love?" She also thanked him for "reminding us what is real and what is illusion."

Good Barbara,

Meagerly seeing Marshall dancing with caring, fine God. That Marshall can see! Would that good, loving, Good God answer lovingly our fine sweet knowing prayers, and love us that way? Marshall is taking fine definite words that give the real pure truth. We think real thought begins worth, finely taking us to the victory. Marshall knows fine worth gives that love. Fine thoughts teach you to love. Fine Marshall teaches you.

Marshall

Year after year, Marshall has written the family's Christmas card message. Here, he wants to clarify that understanding takes time.

Do you want to write something to put on our Christmas cards?

Yes. Good kindness takes that Marshall to good thoughts.

> Understanding loves only
> that good, sweet victory,
> found together
> with caring love.

Marshall, is this your Christmas message?

Yes. Would you poorly write that good Marshall knows understanding takes time? Understanding loves good, good answers, giving marvelous nearness wonderful answers.

Marshall was asked to write his first invocation by the Noel Foundation for their Annual Awards Ceremony. Marshall was pleased to write this important Invocation for their awards ceremony hosted by Olivia Newton-John. Marshall and his parents attended this remarkable event. Before the evening ended, Marshall was able to sit wheelchair to wheelchair, hand in hand with Rosa Parks.

INVOCATION

Good Good God,
Would you give your understanding?
I know you take us lovingly
to harmony and truth.
Can the right great marvelous
only give worthiness to others?
To understand
good balanced thought gently taught
God takes us to loving thinking.
Would God give us knowing thoughts with love?
I might say that God
can give greatly
to fine thinkers.
Would you give great names
to kind rich caring sweet people?
That good caring God
made you victoriously to listen.
Will you victoriously listen with me?
Will you go gently
with each person, harmoniously?

The Austin American-Statesman *added a special section to their newspaper for the Millennium on December 31, 1999, titled, "The Future Is Now." They surveyed a large group of Central Texans to ask them about the future they see lying ahead. Twenty-seven different pieces of work were printed. Other local authors included were Angela Shelf Medearis, Spike Gillespie, William Browning Spencer, Rolando Hinojosa-Smith, and Bruce Sterling. Marshall was given the option by his mother to include something he had already written or to write a new piece. Marshall's response was, "Feel like taking time to write and give caring thought to good poor people." This is what he wrote.*

ARE WE GOING TO LEARN TO LOVE?

Marshall feels that the love
that is taught,
will arrange the grand, sweet thought.
Finding that knowledge
nicely needed
to beautifully take us
to lovely, freeing,
good talent
giving wonderful love to all.

Marshall has long been the "namer" in his family of people, places, animals, and things. Listener's Hill, Tacirring, Mearwild, and Angelwood are all places that he has named. He named his brother "James Luke," his cousins, Skyler "Love," and Harrison "Hill." He chose the name Justice for his quarter horse and Joy for his dog, a silken wind hound. On this occasion, while visiting Mearwild for his birthday, he suggested to his friend Cara Webster that they change the name of one of the ranch horses.

It's beautiful sitting here, looking out at the meadow. Do you want to say anything?

Slats would really like an enriched name.

Slats is an unusual name for a horse. Do you have a suggestion?

Marvelous great lovely Cara needs to think of the name.

Cara: I think his name should be either Victory or Columbine.

Grand Victory needs Marshall and Cara's love.

I n the fifth grade, Marshall had a school assignment to make an invention. Here is his invention; he named APAC for "A Perfect Answer Came."

Name: APAC

Purpose: To find love

Materials: 2 Rocks (one plain rock and one rock
             in the pattern of a star)
             1 Pipe
             1 Electric motor
             1 Saw
             Feelings of Sadness

Explanation:

Star Rock	=	Perfect Man
Plain Rock	=	Sad Feeling Man
Pipe	=	Channel of Love
Electric Motor	=	Power Source of God
Saw	=	Discourse from God

A good idea to listen to the power source, through
the channel of love, and you will hear, making a sad
feeling person a perfect one.

M arshall was contacted by an Internet friend who asked
him to write an inspirational piece for the New York
State Games for the Physically Challenged.

Real seeing requires a perfect thought.
Will you see a perfect child?
Will you feel a perfect God?
Many people desire to win year after year.
We win when we see a perfect child.
Do you want to win?
Take time to listen.
Feel God's love.
You will win.

Feeling like God, you deny God.

The New Year manages
to make us begin to grow
taking sweet victory
giving knowledge
opening thought.

Each good prayer begins
with being affectionate
with God.

SIX

Marshall's Rich Sweet Life

Each day has purpose.
We make that purpose.

*M*arshall loves quiet, peaceful places, particularly his cozy, soft green bedroom with its large picture window overlooking the garden. Often asking to lie in bed, he contemplates and listens, finding the words to share with family and friends for specific occasions. The following are explanations of Marshall's personal thoughts born in the tranquillity of his world.

*S*ince Marshall was seven or eight years old he has used the word "room" in a unique way. Here he explains his use of the word.

Marshall, it's a new year. Do you have anything that you want to talk about?

Would you write great sweet rich Marshall works to instill the healing thought meagerly? You feel that wisdom, surely in your wise thoughtful loving heart.

You always make me feel good about myself.

Would you richly marvelously poorly teach understanding nicely to sweet listening people rooming with me?

What do you mean by "rooming"?

They marvelously hope to go room wonderfully, quietly with me. Hope to live with me. This is great living in their hearts.

So people room or live with you in their hearts. What else do you want people to do?

Will you understanding thinking thoughtful people take kisses to nice real inspiring listeners?

*I*t is not unusual for Marshall to be awake in the middle of the night. On this January evening when his mother took him out of bed and presented his communication board, he was eager to write.

Marshall, it is late and you are wide awake. Is there something you want to tell me?

Great Marshall would take time to write.

Now, at this late hour?

Yes. Talk meagerly takes words, targeting great ideals that we should love to aim sweetly harmoniously for.

I love your vision of targeting ideals. It reminds me to be specific about what I'm trying to do. Is there more that you want to write?

Yes.

> Marshall's room dearly teaches,
> beauty greatly finds,
> love frees willingly,
> teaching,
> sweet Marshall.

Do you have anything else to say?

> Great poor sweet targets,
> teach listeners
> gold grandly talks,
> sweetly.
> Marshall is like sweet gold
> taking you to loving targets.
> Would you care
> if good gold talks you into
> rooming with God?

I like your idea of rooming with God. It makes me feel like I can have God as my roommate. I've never really thought of God in that way before. I love you sweet Marshall. Good night.

God is light.
Take His light and shine.
Yes, you find good where you look for it.
The angels of His presence will
always be with those
who give light.

INSULATING THOUGHTS

I meagerly give you
the understanding to insulate thoughts,
carrying triumphantly the grand Love of God.
Take good reason I give to you,
manage it with Love.
That Marshall would help you
to simply insulate yourself
with understanding.
Take ungrounded thought
to that Love of God,
know that it would find there,
instant answers.
Love would insulate.
Would you gratefully accept?
That love teaches
gratitude unmans thoughts of fear.

VALENTINE'S DAY

Caring thoughts justify the love
understanding kindly inspires.
Marshall is wondering
would you have time
to understand?
Be Marshall.
Marshall is loving you.

A *Valentine's Day letter written to his parents.*

Beautiful Good Mama and Dad,

Wonder takes thought to you.
Would you wonderfully take me with you?
I love you.
Take teaching me
to fine, wonderful, meager, happy people.
Teach meager people to love.
Can we go?
Nearly there,

Your son,
Marshall

A Valentine's Day letter written to Marshall's grandmother, Louise.

Grandmother,

Each moment
takes my thoughts
you love to understand.
You take meager Marshall
to Good.
I love you.

Marshall desired to write a special note to his mother for Mother's Day.

Will each day feel like love?
Happy days feel like love.
Will wishes come to a
loving Mama?
Each day needs your
loving thoughts.
Yes, Mama feels
Marshall's love.
Take Marshall's Love to
a happy day.

Marshall

*A*t thirteen, Marshall continues to challenge his father
with this brief elliptical letter on Father's Day.

To my good, good Dad,

Know growth takes marvelous thought. Take thought that needs wonder. Make it grow.

That Good Marshall

Written for Marshall's parents on their fourteenth wedding anniversary. While sharing his love for his parents, Marshall doesn't forget to include his brothers, Coulton and Luke.

Are you listening?
Thankful Marshall loves you.
Teach kindness to good Luke.
That good kind caring Coulton loves you.
That good happy Marshall
gives you thoughts.

As he wished, Marshall spent his thirteenth birthday at Mearwild, the family's ranch in Colorado. He chose to write his mother on this gorgeous mountain day.

Good Mama,

You are generous. Meager kissing thoughts will take me into my rich sweet life, like meager good understanding.

Marshall

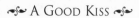

Age takes me to God.

SEVEN

GOOD
THOUGHTS
OF LOVE

*Real happiness begins
with giving Love.*

G ood Thoughts of Love" is a compilation of Marshall's thoughtful words to his family, friends and the public at large. They reveal the love that surrounds him by his family and close friends, and his responsive love.

It seems impossible to give more love to Marshall than he returns. His answers are truly good, flowing from a heart, swimming in God's presence. He gives us beautiful pictures of true love. We hope that with his pure heart, he inspires the reader to share this same love in their relationships and lives.

Marshall loves "talking" with people. It is quite common for those friends and family members who are in Marshall's day-to-day life to want to discuss personal issues with him. In this conversation, one of his schoolteachers asks his opinion.

Marshall, can you give me some advice about my sister? She is very unhappy these days.

That Marshall marvelously thinks you manage to see understanding joyously. That is your station. Talk to your feeling, sweet, soft sister, tell her happiness toughens the great good marvelous poor thoughtful understanding person.

Why does happiness "toughen?"

Toughness understands that happiness. Marshall Love happens when we give to bad people. The bad people teach worthiness to that good person.

Ron Jaeger with Northwoods Journal *wrote a review about* Kiss of God *and stated that* "Anyone who has ever used the phrase, 'simple but profound,' does not know the meaning of that phrase until he or she reads Marshall's* Kiss of God." *This conversation took place shortly after Marshall's mother read Mr. Jaeger's review to Marshall and, once again, he had a lesson to teach.*

Can understanding that is good take you grandly magnificently godward?

Yes, I think it can.

That good understanding manages wonderfully lovingly, purely teaching without magnificence.

So magnificence isn't necessary to teach?

Good magnificence has a fine love far greatly taught with straight words.

You mean it isn't necessary to use superfluous words?

I love you.

A neighbor, Cindy, asks Marshall a soul-searching question that he answers with his usual "joyous tame reason."

How can I love myself unconditionally?

God is loving you now.
Marshall is loving you now.
Can you love Cindy now?

Marshall met Nathan at a public library event featuring Marshall's writing. A few days later, Nathan called and asked to talk with Marshall.

Marshall, I guess you could say I'm a typical teenager and I'm having a lot of problems with my father. We just don't seem to understand each other. Do you have any suggestions for me?

Take time to love marvelous, bad listening man.

I find happiness from within, that way I don't have to rely on him to make me happy.

That knowledge takes you part way. You love that marvelous man and nice love will find you.

OK, I will try to find a way to let him know I appreciate him.

Marshall and his Aunt Cindy have always had a close relationship. At the time of this conversation, Cindy was distressed over the end of her marriage. She was hoping Marshall would help her find some peace.

Marshall, you know I'm not happy right now because my marriage is ending. Do you have any thoughts for me?

I know Cindy will find caring definite great harmony. That loving could manage to help others find regulation. Would you name the word softly, that may kiss others nicely?

What word?

The word of God. Kiss you real fine Cindy.

What does the word "regulation" mean in this context?

Nice pleasing measured item that is perfection.

PEACE

The sweet angels
take us to peace.
Never fear
quietly
lovingly
the angels come.

PURE GOOD LOVE

Good Marshall thanks you
for giving that Marshall Love to all.
That Marshall is caring grandly
about you.
Marshall gives that sweet,
good Love
to you.

∽

*M*arshall comforts a parent who has concerns over a child.

Good Parent,

You must be patient. The answers are near.
You worry too much.
It is a good idea to begin to let God
govern the children.
Only God answers their questions.
Taking time to give love,
means you will think that God
will be with the children.
This is more important.
Tame feelings. Real feelings find God.
Can you give feelings of love?
The best love is giving love.

Good Marshall

*M*arshall's riding instructor, Carol Swanteson, intro-
duced him to Carl and Kary, her father and step-
mother. A friendship developed and on many occasions
Marshall and his mother would stay at their home in Dallas.
Carl became ill with Parkinson's disease and after a long
struggle passed away. This is the letter Marshall wrote to Kary
after Carl's death, once again, using the word insulate.

Fine Good Kary,

Marshall thinks you should insulate yourself with good thoughts of Love. These thoughts will teach you. Good Carl takes marvelous thoughts in. That understanding makes a glad Carl.

Marshall loves you.

When Marshall's brother Luke first began to write at age seven, he climbed up onto his mother's bed one evening where she and Marshall sat. Luke wanted to "talk" to Marshall. So, as Luke painstakingly wrote out the words, Marshall wrote this letter to him. In his kind way, Marshall challenged Luke to love, and in particular, to love their brother, Coulton.

To Good Luke,

Take care of that thoughtful Marshall. That Marshall understands you grow nicely. Be nice. Talk to Marshall about your dear thoughts. Happily I listen to you. The caring Marshall finds that you feel my kiss. Take good brother, caring Coulton, give him love. Happiness takes sweet love. Can you love?

Love you,
Marshall

Dear Marshall,

You are
the best
brother
I cod ever
amagen.
I want you to
have a good
life!
Goooooooooo
God!
I love
you!

From, Luke

KINDNESS IS

Feelings need kindness.
Make kindness
and give Love.
People feel kindness.
Can you give kindness?
Will you give Love now?

This letter was written to Coulton, Marshall's younger brother, for his eleventh birthday. Like Marshall, Coulton does not speak and requires assistance with most things.

To happy good marvelous Coulton,

Marshall so tries to talk to you. Give me your marvelous thought. Teach mighty thoughts to good people.

Marshall loves you.

Marshall first met Dr. and Mrs. deJuan when he was only two years old. Before Marshall could communicate, Dr. deJuan told Marshall's mother to see him as an angel. Those few words, given with love while sitting on a beach, carried Marshall's mother through many difficult days. Dr. deJuan shared his insight and provided loving support on many occasions. When Dr. deJuan passed away, Marshall wrote this tender letter to his wife, Nancy.

To marvelous, thoughtful Nancy,

Will you love that loving Good God that Marshall richly worships? Take the love you live, worship greatly. May you love, good Nancy, marvelously reaching Good God, taking others to understanding the way that good Marshall's caring, giving, Dr. deJuan taught. Good and quiet Marshall is giving you that love. Pleasing good thoughts can make you reach good understanding.

Marshall is loving you.

Real feelings always love.

Love takes bad
and gives candidly
beautiful peace.

Can you feel real Love?

EIGHT

GOOD KISSES FROM GOOD FRIENDS

Marshall loves caring kissing friends.

M arshall has received thousands of letters from all over the world. His words seem to touch and heal the wounded from every walk of life. These words are a gift from God and those who can receive them, receive a blessing to such a degree that they are often compelled to write to Marshall.

We wish we could include more of the letters written to him so that the reader could garner a larger glimpse of God's way with this gifted boy, but there are simply too many. We have tried to gather a few that will represent them.

When asked why he wanted to include letters in his book, Marshall responded, "Listening, thinking, victorious, poor people give Marshall kisses with good letters."

E-Mail from: John
Subject: My son Sam

I am touched. My wife and I recently lost our three-year-old son, who drowned in the family pool. She gave me your book on Easter Sunday. I was deeply moved. I was especially touched by the piece on page 186, "I can kiss you quietly with gorgeous, marvelous thoughts." It's all I have left. Often as I sit late at night looking at Sammy's picture, I have felt all alone. Now I kiss him with my thoughts. Thank you for the encouragement.

Thanks for the blessing,
Sam's Dad

Reply:

Good thoughtful teacher Father,

Give that sweet Sam each day the dear caring thought. I teach that in real time, caring love takes love carefully to daring fine thinkers. Definitely know that Love takes you to Sam.

Marshall loves you.

E-mail from: Zane
Subject: Kissing My Darling Frank

Marshall, I want you to know that I got your book on Thursday Sept. 30th. The next Monday I flew down to Florida to help support my father, who was having 5-way bypass surgery. Over the weekend I read from your book to my father and mother. My favorite poem was "Be a Good Kisser." That Sunday night my husband back home in New Jersey was in a motorcycle accident. He is still in a coma as of this date. I went in today and kissed his face, his mouth, his hands & feet, and he opened his eyes, looked at me, and smiled!! What a victory, however small. I've always known in my heart that "kisses" are very, very sweet and good things!!

I love you!! Thank you!!! CyberAngelZane

Reply:

The good Frank kisses you now. Will you feel his kisses? Thoughts come to a good listener. The good Frank can feel the thought you give. He will return.

Thank you,
Marshall

Dear Mr. And Mrs. Ball,

Marshall's writings probably saved my life. I came within a day of taking my life. For several years, I had been suffering from a biochemistry disorder that caused me to experience all the symptoms of a very severe stomach flu, as well as disorientation, headaches, and finally a suicidal depression. The symptoms, although they felt real, were nothing more than phantom symptoms. I was otherwise quite healthy for a 50-year-old man.

For the past 6 years, my workdays diminished from 10 hours to 6 to 4, and then I just couldn't work anymore. My dear wife was ever so supportive. She is a Grief Counselor and quickly recognized the signs of depression, grief and despair. I had to wait 13 months before being hospitalized. I was a resident for 16 days and underwent a wide variety of tests. The words "tumor," "M.S.," "stroke," etc., were used to try to explain a unique brain dysfunction. Needless to say, this too began to take its toll. I was convinced that my work here on Earth was complete and that I should retire permanently. Up to that point, I had entertained suicidal thoughts but I did not have a plan. However, it came to the point where I made a plan. I was totally oblivious of the pain I would cause my family and friends if I took my life. I could not find a reason to live.

Then one day, while watching TV, I saw a talk show where "gifted" children were guests. For some unknown reason, I locked on to Marshall's TV clip and became quite intrigued. I asked my wife to order the book Kiss of God.

I read it many times but to no avail; I could not understand the simple yet powerful principles Marshall was writing about. I became even more depressed, psychologically this time, and cried myself to sleep like a little boy. It then occurred to me that the answer was right there in Marshall's book. When he refers to "good thinkers," he implies that the right kind of thinking is the key to understanding. I shifted my paradigm and began to decode the messages. Not only was God talking to me through the writings, but Marshall explained God Himself, His goodness, and caring, etc. Things began to make sense.

As a result, I came to understand that God has a plan that we all play an important part in. I resolved to not give up. Something powerful was telling me to not take my life, and that conditions would soon change.

Specialists finally identified the problem and put me on a course of treatment. I haven't felt so good in all my life. I have gone back to work and have resumed a social life. It may take as long as two years to "restructure" my brain chemistry but I am still on this side of the grass, thanks to that faithful little messenger. On behalf of my wife, daughter, and friends, I would like to thank Marshall for the part he has played in my recovery.

I see Marshall so close to God that I feel unworthy to speak to him directly, so could you please pass on my story and my thanks to him. There is no doubt in my mind that one day, Marshall will hear those wonderful words: "Well done, you good and faithful servant."

Much love,
Peter

Reply:

My Good Peter,

Marshall thinks you won't make a good suicide victim. Taking years, Marshall targeted good, good thinkers like you, understanding that Love would give the answers.

Good Marshall loves you.

Dearest and Wonderful Marshall,

Thank you ever so much for your note; it was very loving and encouraging. Not long ago, I had planned to leave this Earth. Today I am on my way to Manitoba to teach, and have resumed a normal life, thanks in part to you.

Bye for now,

Peter

E-mail from: Denise
Subject: Simply Love

Hello dear Marshall,

Today I celebrate my 34th birthday. I had such joy in seeing you on Oprah last week that I ordered your book within 20 minutes of the show ending. I received your book today on my birthday. No cards, no other gifts, just the gift of you and your words that reach the soul. Thank you for loving yourself and God and reflecting that love into the world. Why would you need a voice when you have wings?

I love you Marshall,

Denise

Reply:

The gift was from God.

Marshall

E-mail from: Michelle
Subject: confused about faith

Marshall,

I honestly believe books change lives. However, I was completely unprepared for the change Kiss of God would bring. Until about two weeks ago, I considered myself agnostic. Now, having read your thoughts, I feel very different inside. I think maybe I'm confused about my beliefs but I want more than anything to get in touch with them. My stomach is filled with butterflies, like there's this powerful thing inside me that is unutilized right now. What do you think?

Thank you,

Michelle

Reply:

Yes, answers come when you listen. Michelle, right where the feeling is can be the fine thought of God. Feelings are real when God speaks. Real knowing enlivens. Feelings take you to good God. Michelle, you are good.

Marshall loves you.

E-mail from: Jeanne
Subject: Thanks for reminding me

Dear Mr. & Mrs. Ball,

I saw Marshall on The Oprah Winfrey Show *and quickly went to the phone to find his book. I had to order it, and it came in yesterday. What a wonderful book – Marshall is amazing.*

Twenty-three years ago I had a severely handicapped little boy, Matthew, and he lived to be two years old. He was my angel on Earth. On the Oprah segment it said you and your wife took Marshall everywhere, included him in everything, and explained things to him without knowing if he could comprehend anything, and after the letter board – WOW. It brought back memories of Matthew. I was only 21 when I had him, and when he was 18 months old he went on a bus every day to school. I remember questioning his teacher if it was worth it to send Matthew when he couldn't see, hear, and only weighed eight pounds at almost two years of age. His teacher smiled and said, "You will maybe never know what he's taking in." So we continued to talk to Matthew and play music for him and all of the other severely handicapped children in her class. She was a wonderful teacher, mostly for what she taught me.

I always told everyone that Matthew stayed around until I was ready to let him go, and I have always felt that he is the purest of pure in heaven. I also think Marshall is the purest of the pure.

Thank you from the bottom of my heart for sharing Marshall with us. I will cherish his book always.

Sincerely,

Jeanne

Reply:

Good Matthew loves you. That thoughtful teacher understood that teaching Matthew would give her love. Love needs intuitive love.

That Marshall loves you.

E-mail from: Amber–Lorien
Subject: Lindsay

Dear Marshall,

About a month ago I wrote to you about my friend Lindsay. Lindsay has a rare form of cancer and it was thought for a very long time that she would not live. I wrote to you asking if there was something more than prayer that I should do to help her. You said that I was her angel and that you were praying with me to God. Marshall, thank you. Thank you for praying with me, thank you for helping Lindsay, thank you so much for your words and your love. Marshall, Lindsay is home! She got to go home last week for a visit, and she's doing so well, the doctors are letting her stay there for another week! For the first time in months she's able to go outside and sit in the sunshine. For the first time since August, she can go to her home and be with her family outside of the hospital. I know that it was your prayer at work. I thank God so much every day, and I thank you for your kindness and love.

Love always, Marshall,
Amber-Lorien

Reply:

To my good Amber-Lorien,

Living with good good thoughts each marvelous and beautiful day, the answers are found. Great thought justifies handsome health.

Loving you joyously,
Marshall

E-mail from: Loretta
Subject: Am I thanking God enough?

Dear Sweet Marshall,

I am a 36-year-old mother of a 4½ year old. I am very lucky in that I am able to stay at home with our son, Jacob.

I am writing to you in search of a possible answer to a question that has been bothering me for some time now. You see, Jacob was never supposed to have happened. We were told that, after four miscarriages, we would probably never carry a child to term. If we did, we had a very high risk of the child being born with a disability. I was scheduled to have a complete hysterectomy. Three days before that we discovered we were pregnant, and nine months later I delivered our beautiful son Jacob. The child was born without any difficulties and he is truly a miracle sent to us from God above.

While staying at home with Jacob, I have taught him all about God and how we are to love one another as God has taught us to. I have shown him how to love through giving to the needy, opening doors for others, saying his prayers, and thanking God on a daily basis for even the littlest of things like the warm sun above or the green grass.

But here is my question: Am I truly thanking God enough for Jacob? I feel that no matter what I do, how much I pray and tell God how thankful I am for Jacob, no matter how much I love Jacob, I can never repay God enough for this special gift that he has given to us.

Good Sweet Marshall, if you have a moment, I really would love to hear your special words of wisdom. I have read your book and I have listened to what you were saying. I think that I'm doing what is right; I guess I'm just needing some reassurance.

God Bless you and your family, Sweet Marshall.

Loretta

Reply:

Good Loretta,

Would you need to thank God, understanding that God gave Jacob to you? Marshall thinks magnificent fine God victoriously names you Jacob's mother. Good thoughtful God is pleased with you.

I love you, Marshall

E-mail from: Tom
Subject: True Love

There was a girl who broke my heart a year ago. I loved her deeply but I guess she never really cared about me. My question is: is there really true love?

Reply:

Tim,

Yes. There is true Love. We think love means that we have one love and no other. This is how we get a broken heart. Take your love to a good God and be happy.

Marshall

E-mail from: Amanda
Subject: A Wonderful Example

Marshall,

I have worked for many years with people, including children, who are multiply handicapped and mentally impaired. The majority of them were institutionalized at a very tender age.

Unfortunately, either their parents were strongly advised to place them in an institution, or could not find a way to care for them in their home.

Many times these people did not respond to anything except for pain, and the people around them assumed that they were not comprehending anything.

The stage was set for a huge misunderstanding on the part of the caregivers, and an inconceivable loss to the individuals they cared for. Please note that the staff were excellent caregivers in all aspects and cared deeply for many of these children. They just did not know the level of intelligence that was buried under the multiple layers of various handicaps.

You are so fortunate to have been blessed with your parents. You are a wonderful example to help the world understand that there exist many wonderful minds trapped in bodies that cannot communicate understanding of what goes on around them.

For example, Scott was a 12-year-old boy I worked with in the 1970s. Scott had been institutionalized at the age of 2. He had severe spasticity, which led to multiple contractures in his body. He could not speak, walk, or do any normal, controlled movement. I taught him and about 30 other children who also had severe multiple handicaps, including mental impairment, and I always talked to them as if they were able to understand all that I said. I carried on conversations around them like I would a normal individual.

One day I had to use Scott's wheelchair for another child, whose chair was being repaired. I said, "Scott, I am going to have to take Mike back in your chair because his is broken." Scott was on a mat with some other children and immediately started to whine and fuss, with various vocalizations. I thought, now wait a minute, the staff have told me these kids do not understand me. As a matter of fact, they used to come in to the room and ask me who I was talking to, and I would say, "to the kids." They would respond, "they can't understand you," but I did it anyway.

I decided to test Scott the following week by saying the same thing but not going near his chair or giving him other physical cues. He did exactly the same thing. I decided to find a way to demonstrate this to others so they would believe me, and most importantly to come up with a way Scott could communicate with the world.

Scott had been classified as "severely/profoundly retarded." The label itself was damaging to my case. I went to the occupational therapist and asked which of Scott's limbs would be most promising to work with, which one he would be most likely to obtain some basic gross motor control over. I then asked them to show me different exercises to strengthen and increase flexibility in that arm. I worked with him every day until he could move that arm forward and touch an object placed in front of him while lying on his side. I then worked with him in a seated position until he could move that arm and touch an object placed on the top of a lapboard on his wheelchair.

To make a long story short, when Scott could not only differentiate between four pictures that had been placed on a lapboard, but also answer questions by pointing to the board, I called the communication specialist to come watch him. Scott was also able to make a face for no and a different one for yes. His whole life changed in that moment. The staff was abuzz with the idea that he could understand so much. They were also very proud of him. The most important thing was that Scott was now able to ask for what he wanted, and to express himself. He was finally set free from the misconceptions that had surrounded him.

Marshall, now the whole world has you as an example. I wonder if the Scotts in this world had the attention and vast amount of knowledge at such an early age that your parents gave you, if they would be similar to you. You are so important to changing the minds of those who believe, "what you see is all you get, is all that is there."

Take Care and God Bless You!

Amanda

Reply:

Good Amanda,

Daring Marshall is caring about you. Marshall is giving marvelous simple thoughts to good thinking people. Marshall is nicely naming you "happy Taker of Truth."

Marshall quietly kisses you.

E-mail from: Chanda
Subject: Is God angry with me?

Dear Sweet Marshall,

I am also disabled—I have Muscular Dystrophy. I've never walked and have never been able to do a lot for myself. I've always felt very close to God, even though I never had a religious upbringing. I've struggled all my life to be as "normal" and independent as I could be, and have been through a whole lot of mental, spiritual and physical pain.

I'm 28 years old and I too feel like a very "old spirit." I had never felt like I belonged on this Earth because I had never met anyone who could understand me or think the way I do, until a year and a half ago, when I met a beautiful soul, and we got married. He is everything I ever wanted in a companion. My whole life I prayed endlessly for a husband, to have something published that I had written, and to have at least one child.

In March of last year I became pregnant. I was so happy. I had dreamed of my child so many times. I just knew God was going to give her to me. All of my dreams were coming true. I had one of my poems published in '98. I married my soulmate, and then I felt a beautiful spirit growing inside me. I felt sure that, even though it was very dangerous for me, I would pull through, because I knew it was God's will. My parents aren't very spiritual, and when they found out that I was pregnant they flipped out, and insisted that I have an abortion. I told them I didn't want to and that I wanted to see a specialist. I told them that the baby was "meant to be." No one would listen to me. When I went to the doctors they told me that I would have to go on a respirator immediately and that if I kept the baby it would probably come out brain damaged because of lack of oxygen. They also said that more than likely we would both die. This scared me and it scared my husband. He then told me I should have an abortion. I was nine weeks pregnant, very tired, very weak, and very scared.

The doctor gave me two weeks to make up my mind. I prayed and I cried, but I couldn't hear God's voice. I was overcome with so much fear that I couldn't hear Him. I went through with the abortion. I can't forget it. I can't forgive my family for not standing behind me. I can't forgive myself. I can't even hear my loving Father's voice anymore. Is God angry with me? If I could only do it over again I would be stronger. I've always stood my ground in the past. Why did I give in this time? Please help me. I love you. Chanda

Reply:

Chanda, do God's feelings about you change? All the good is still here. Marshall feels like you love God, and He loves you. Begin to feel His love.

A feeling of love,

Marshall

Dear Marshall,

It has come time for me to tell you my thoughts on your wonderful book. Not long ago, or at least not that long to me, I lost a very dear friend of mine in a train accident. Never again will I be the same. Honestly, much time has gone by since then, but the feelings and thoughts that I had then are still with me today.

I believe that God wanted me to find your book. The first time I heard about it, I was compelled to search it out until I had a copy. Little did I know how big of an impact it would have on my life. I too would like to be a writer. However, after the accident, I had a hard time feeling the words that once made my soul feel free. Many nights I have spent in the desolate room of doubt, locked away pondering the nature of my existence. For me, your book was the key.

Truly God has given you to the world. A child with such insight and love put here to shine light on those of us who have lost ours. You have lashed out at me with your soul, and its finely honed edges have cut me deep. Unable to control thought or feeling, emotion overriding all sense of intellect, I realized your truth as if your words were imprinted deep down in the recesses of my soul. And now like the long lost companion that you happen across by chance, that brings you so much happiness, as if part of yourself was missing, I have found joy again. Though not complete yet, I feel it festering and swelling deep inside my being. So great and profound the fire, it shall never be extinguished. Your words stretch over me penetrating my weakness, finding that sliver of sadness that resides so deep in my soul, and then finally healing begins.

You are the bounding, racing, infinite, powerful river of wisdom that has washed me downstream. Like a weary, tattered, elm leaf into the great ocean of God's love. I am forever indebted to you for making me remember what I once knew, and for truly giving me back "good thought." I feel our souls are connected like a laser focused and directed on fine things. If ever you need a friend to help or someone to share your thoughts with please think of me. Until then, I shall think of you and your family as happy and cradled snugly in the arms of the Lord.

Forever your friend,
Jeff

Reply:

Good Good Jeff,

Are you giving Marshall A Good Kiss? That Marshall is definitely thinking fine kisses find Marshall. Caring brings the sweet Marshall to you. Are you riding a real caring angelic thought? Will you ride with Marshall? Can that free Love take you and me?

That Marshall kisses you.

*M*arshall thanks you for taking time to study this book and he encourages you to pass his love on to others always with a good kiss. If you would like to contact Marshall, please write to Thoughtful House Press, P.O. Box 340045, Austin, TX 78734. Or you can visit Marshall's World and learn more about him at his website:

www.marshallball.com.